Who Is Missing?

Linda Ekblad
Illustrated by Gwen Connelly

The animals come to the party.

Cat comes. Who is missing?

Dog comes back.
Who is missing?

Lamb comes back.
Who is missing?

Hen comes back.
Who is missing?

Monkey comes back.
Who is missing?

Pig is back.
No one is missing!